UNDERSTANDING THE CHINESE BUDDHIST TEMPLE
Karma Yönten Gyatso

SUMERU

UNDERSTANDING THE CHINESE BUDDHIST TEMPLE

Karma Yönten Gyatso

COVER: Altar cloth on the chanting master's lectern, in front of the main shrine, facing the congregation.

The Chinese characters read:

> THE DHARMAKAYA RECEIVES THE INCENSE CLOUD

The photographs in this book were taken by the author, at the Ching Kwok Chinese Buddhist Temple in Toronto in 2009 and 2010.

We are grateful to the Venerable Wu De, abbot, for his kind assistance with the explanations found herein.

Conceived, photographed, written,
designed and produced by
John Negru, writing as
Karma Yönten Gyatso

Published by
The Sumeru Press Inc.
PO Box 2089, Richmond Hill, Ontario
Canada L4E 1A3

ॐ SUMERU

ISBN 978-1-896559-06-3
First print edition

For more information about
The Sumeru Press Inc.
visit us at

www.sumeru-books.com

For Gung Gung

Ching Kwok
"Complete Enlightenment"
Chinese Buddhist Temple

Toronto, Ontario

Introduction

CHING KWOK (*Complete Enlightenment*) Temple was originally established in Toronto in 1992 as Tai Bay (*Great Compassion*) Temple, in a small and somewhat nondescript building at 930 Dundas Street West.

Some years later, the temple expanded in its new location at 300 Bathurst Street with its new name. The building was originally built as a movie theatre and in subsequent years it had served as an Eastern Orthodox church when that part of Toronto was home to many inhabitants from eastern Europe.

Toronto's Chinatown has expanded enormously since its humble beginnings near the intersection of Dundas and Bay Streets. The first satellite community sprang up about a kilometre west on Dundas Street at Spadina Avenue in the late 1960s. Chinese Canadian communities now find homes in Mississauga, Markham, Riverdale and other parts of the Greater Toronto Area.

Although many waves of Asian immigrants have come to Toronto since then and moved on to more affluent neighbourhoods after settlement, Dundas Street West continues to be a vibrant hub for the city's Chinese and Vietnamese residents, as well as for the wider community who appreciate the neighbourhood's many delights.

It is within this context that we present this book about Ching Kwok Buddhist Temple, as part of our series of monographs about Canadian Buddhist temples from all traditions and heritages.

Many westerners have become Buddhist practitioners since the 1960s. For those who follow other traditions, it is valuable to have an opportunity to understand the iconography of Mahayana Chinese Buddhist temples, since so much of what we have come to know in the West as "Buddhism" is filtered through that lens.

Finding common ground is an essential of Buddhist practice. In fact, reverence for the Sangha, or practicing community, is one of the Three Jewels, along with the Buddha and the Dharma. There is no room for sectarian ego.

For spiritual seekers of all faiths who simply find the atmosphere of a Mahayana Chinese Buddhist temple to be a calm and uplifting place, but who may themselves have little or no previous experience with Buddhism, the statues and images there can be exotic and mysterious. Words are not needed to experience their power. But be that as it may, the opportunity to understand what lies behind those icons – their meanings – is an open gateway to even greater awareness.

— ❧ —

WITHIN the Chinese Buddhist Temple, traditionally one will find seven Halls: the Great Hero Hall (where the main Buddha statues are found); the Hall of Meditation; the Hall of the Five Observations (also known as the Eating Hall); the Tripitaka Hall (the temple's library); the Sleeping Hall; the Teaching Hall; and the Field of Pagodas (where teachers and residents are buried). These are, of necessity, considerably modified in the Canadian context.

Within the limitations of its physical venue, Ching Kwok Temple follows a full liturgical schedule. Each day, prayers and sutras are chanted at 5:30 am and 4:00 pm. Saturday services are held from 2:00 - 4:00 pm. Two Saturdays each month, the theme of the service is reciting the names of the Buddha. Two Saturdays each month, the theme is reciting the sutras. Once a month there is a full-day and full-night Saturday service where congregants are able to observe the Eight Precepts. On Sundays from 10:00 am - 12:00 pm there is chanting, followed by a Dharma Talk. Throughout the year, a wide variety of special ceremonies and activities also take place.

The material in this book is organized as a walk-around.

The first images deal with the overall layout of the temple and close-ups of the main altar icons. Next are images of the Dharma Protectors on either side of the main shrine. Various instruments associated with services are next. The shrine near the front door, dedicated to Guanyin, the Bodhisattva of Compassion, follows. Next, the remembrance wall, several offering tables and the rear chapel are included. We finish with images of Dharma sayings on the walls, decorative panels, and views as one leaves the hall.

Each of the photographs is accompanied by a brief explanation based on my subsequent conversations with Ven. Wu De, head monk at the temple, with translation by Ven. Ivan Trinh for one interview and Ms. Chris Ng for another, supplemented by my further research. Their willingness to go through all the photographs and provide the context behind the images is greatly appreciated.

My thanks are also extended to Professor Henry Shiu, University of Toronto Scarborough Department of Humanities, who graciously translated some of the more complex ideograms presented here.

Forgiveness is requested from the reader for any errors and omissions. I am not a Buddhist scholar, merely a traveller on the path. The responsibility for errors is mine.

— ❧ —

PLEASE consider visiting to see our other Dharma titles and free e-books at our website www.sumeru-books.com if you have enjoyed this book.

MAIN SHRINE ROOM: This photo was taken from in front of the incense offering table just inside the front door. We are facing west. The three Buddhas on the main shrine are, from left to right, Amituo Fo (Amitabha, the Buddha of Infinite Light), Shi Jia Mou Ni Fo (Shakyamuni, the historical Buddha) and Yaoshi Fo (Bhaisajyaguru, the Medicine Buddha). In front of the shrine are offering tables. On either side of the shrine are the Dharma Protectors. On the right can be seen the remembrance wall. On the left is the entrance to the Hall of Virtue chapel.

LEFT PILLAR → Detail

The Buddha in his *Nirmanakaya* body with boundless compassion teaches his disciples; let the hearers put an end to their delusion and sufferings, realizing truth and happiness.

RIGHT PILLAR
Detail ←

In the period of Dharma decline, the community aspires to the (ordained) Sangha with virtues and wisdom for leadership and renewal.

MAIN SHRINE

AMITUO FO
Amitabha Buddha

Buddha of Infinite Light, Lord of the Western Paradise. In this representation, his right hand is in the mudra gesture of teaching, while his left hand rests in meditative repose.

SHI JIA MOU NI FO
Shakyamuni Buddha

Buddha of the Auspicious Aeon. In this representation, his hands are in the mudra of meditation. The three smaller statues in front of the main statue are also images of Shakyamuni Buddha.

The three large statues were made in Macau, with painted gold leaf on Burmese mahogany, a particularly resilient wood. The wood is covered with layers of cloth and special lacquers before the gold leaf is applied.

YAOSHI FO
Bhaisajyaguru Buddha

The Medicine Buddha. In this representation, his hands hold the Treasure Pagoda, where healing herbs are mixed and prepared.

MANY BUDDHAS
Main altar

Combining multiple images of Buddhas on a shrine is common practice in all Buddhist traditions. It is oft-repeated as a symbol that there are countless Buddhas and countless Buddha-lands. The Mahayana sutras typically begin with homage to the Buddhas of the Ten Directions and the Three Times. This is a visual representation of the Mahayana philosophy so eloquently expounded in the Lotus Sutra (Ch: *Fa Hua Jing*, Skt: *Saddharma Pundarika Sutra*).

In the aura of the main statue, smaller Buddhas can be seen in relief among the tendrils and flames. This is another common motif. Variations in images of Bodhisattvas and revered teachers can include images of lineage teachers, tutelary deities, or other Buddhas and Bodhisattvas associated with the same Buddha Family.

SHAKYAMUNI'S PARINIRVANA: Lord Buddha always recommended that practitioners sleep on their right sides as this was most conducive to healthy and insightful rest. When Lord Buddha himself passed away into Nirvana, he lay down on his right side and gave his last advice to his disciples – strive diligently to realize your own innate Buddha Nature. Images of the Buddha in the reclining pose have come to represent that transition and threefold teaching; that all conditioned things are subject to dissolution; that Nirvana is real; and that The Buddha actually accomplished the realization of it. On the seated

Behind is a statue of Shakyamuni seated in meditation. On the seated Buddha's chest can be seen a Svastika (Skt: *sva* = self-arisen; *tika* = mark), the ancient Indian symbol for the Wheel of the Law. Both metal statues were made in Taiwan. Behind them is another statue of Shakyamuni in meditation, carved in Burmese white alabaster. Surrounding them are offerings of a candle, persimmons and mangoes.

SHI JIA MOU NI FO
Shakyamuni Buddha

The historical Buddha, seated in full lotus meditation posture, holding a begging bowl.

Full lotus posture involves crossing the legs with both soles up. For practitioners in half lotus, only the left leg is placed up. In either case, the hands are folded in the lap with the thumbs lightly touching. According to Buddhist psychology, the right side is active (Ch: *yang*) and the left side is receptive (Ch: *yin*). The Buddha is depicted with his right hand above, symbolizing his attainment of enlightenment and subsequent active teaching. Practitioners normally place the left hand above the right hand. The touching thumbs balance, focus and amplify this energy. In meditation, the eyes are open, gazing down.

The begging bowl is symbolic of the Buddha's renunciation of a householder life. Buddhist monks and nuns are expected to devote their energy to practice, teaching and good works. They rely on the kindness of the laity for their support and do not engage in business for personal profit. On a deeper level, the empty begging bowl is said to hold the elixir of ultimate reality.

Buddha is sitting on a lotus throne, surmounted by sun and moon disks (not visible). His form is healthy, showing his choice of the Middle Way as opposed to the extreme of asceticism. The enlarged ear lobes are symbolic of his royal upbringing, since royals of that time and place wore earrings which would stretch the lobes. Enlarging, rather than elongating, the ear lobes is a particularly Chinese artistic style of representation.

Around his physical appearance body (Skt: *Nirmanakaya*), he is surrounded by a body aura representing the bliss body (Skt: *Sambhogakaya*) and a mind aura symbolizing the truth body (Skt: *Dharmakaya*). The centre of the mind aura is a spotless mirror – the clear wisdom of ultimate reality. His hands are folded at the midriff energy centre (Skt: *chakra*). At the heart chakra is a svastika. At the throat chakra are three folds, at the forehead chakra is a crystal. At the crown chakra is a red painted topknot. The "buddha bump" above the crown chakra symbolizes Buddha's transcendence of everyday reality and accomplishment of supernatural realms.

The statue, made in Taiwan in the Chinese artistic style, is burnished copper alloy, with three types of gold surface treatment and polychrome painted highlights on the head. The base is decorated with symmetrical floral motifs. It is about 25 cm tall.

Shi Jia Mou Ni Fo
Shakyamuni Buddha

The historical Buddha, in the posture known as "Calling the Earth to Witness." This is the pose of the Buddha immediately after attaining Highest Perfect Enlightenment at dawn on the morning following the full moon in May, under the Bodhi tree in Bodh-Gaya, India. The left hand is in meditation, the place from which Buddha has come. The right hand is touching the ground, confirming and expressing the reality of his insight. His eyes are open and engaging. He is seated on a lotus throne. The statue is made of Burmese white alabaster with gold and polychrome paint in the Burmese style. It is about one meter tall. The hands and feet are enlarged to compensate for the fragility of the stone. The elongated ears are made stronger by connecting them to the shoulders.

Shi Jia Mou Ni Fo
Shakyamuni Buddha

The historical Buddha, seated in meditation posture. This is the central statue on the main altar. It is made of Burmese mahogany, covered in layers of resin-soaked cloth for shaping, and then painted with gold leaf. Buddha's hair is traditionally depicted as blue – a colour originally achieved by grinding lapis lazuli for the pigment.

The statue is about three meters tall. The auras are painted an auspicious red, so beloved by Chinese artists. Note the mirror in the head aura.

On the right you can see part of a dragon. There are four dragons on the main altar, wrapped around pillars on either side of each statue, supporting a decorative pavillion roof. According to Chinese mythology, the dragon represents power and wrathful energy in a protective role. While the five-toed dragon is usually associated with Imperial power, it is here in its four-toed role as a Dharma protector. In its front right paw it clutches the celestial pearl.

AMITUO FO

Amitabha Buddha

The Buddha of Infinite Light

Lord of the Western Pure Land (Skt: *Sukhavati*), seated in teaching posture. His right hand is in the gesture of expelling demons (Skt: *karana mudra*), while his left hand remains in meditation pose symbolizing his continued clear awareness while teaching. Resting in his left hand is a jewel box symbolizing the precious teaching.

Pure Land Buddhism is one of the most widely-practiced Mahayana traditions. It is especially strong in Vietnam, China and Japan. In Pure Land Buddhism, Amitabha is the central figure of devotional practice. Amitabha's vows included creating a Pure Land where beings could practice the dharma with no hindrance, promising that anyone who merely called upon him with reverence would be reborn in that Pure Land upon leaving this one.

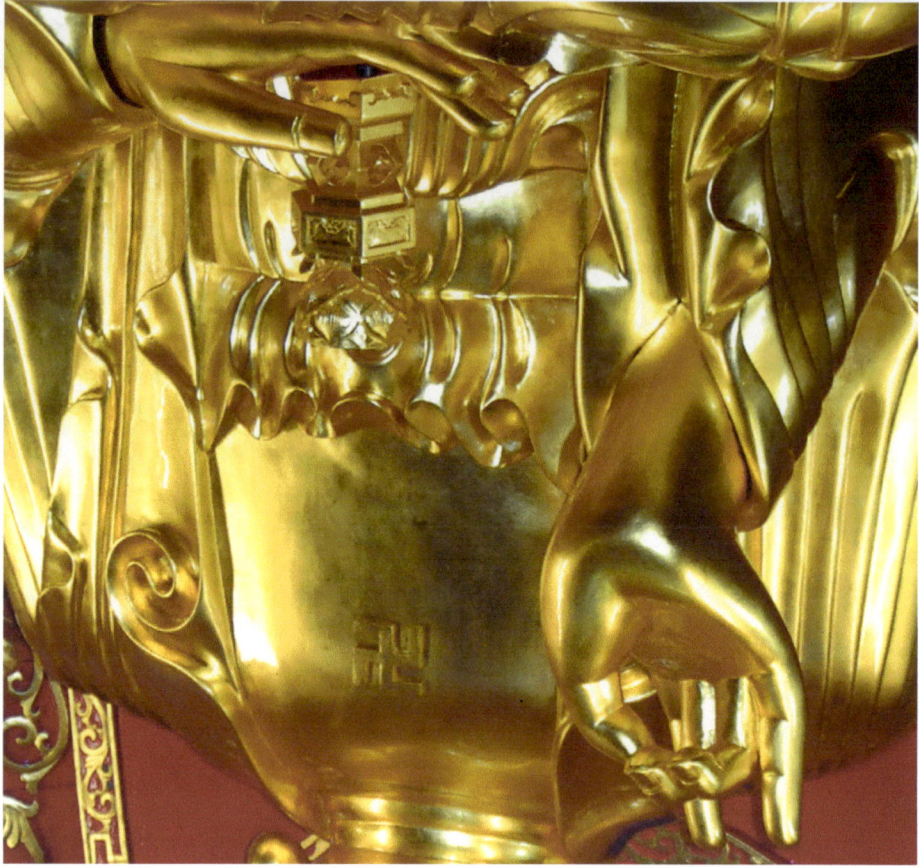

Wenshu Pusa

Manjusri

Bodhisattva of Wisdom

This wooden statue depicts Wenshu in the mode of a scholar seated in a rocky bamboo grove, holding a sutra in his right hand and with his left hand in the gesture of teaching. This teaching gesture with the thumb touching the middle finger is also sometimes known as the heart mudra, a centering force. His left leg is extended, in what is known as the relaxed princely pose.

The statue is about 1.5 metres tall. It is in front of the main statue of Amituo Fo on the left side of the main altar.

Yaoshi Fo
Bhaisajyaguru Buddha
Medicine Buddha

Resting in his right hand is the treasure pagoda where his healing herbs and potions are mixed. His left hand is in the karana mudra - expelling demons. Flanking Shakyamuni, Bhaisajyaguru here is modeled as an almost mirror image of the Amitabha statue on the left of the shrine.

In front is a wooden statue of Guanyin (Avalokitesvara, the Bodhisattva of Compassion, portrayed with a thousand hands and a thousand eyes).

The throne upon which a Buddha sits if often referred to as the "Lion Throne." In this photo, you can see one of the four Foo Lions at each of the corners of the throne. The male lion is shown with a ball, symbolizing the flower of life, under his right front paw. In front of the throne, slightly lower and to the left, is a railing newel post surmounted by a Foo Dog finial. Foo Dogs are a frequent decorative motif in Chinese mythology – symbolizing the faithful protective companion.

Guanyin
Avalokesvara
Bodhisattva of Compassion

This wooden statue depicts Guanyin in the mode of having a thousand heads and a thousand hands. Each head sees the suffering of beings in a different world, and each hand reaches out to assist them in their individual journey to happiness and enlightenment. While the ultimate nature of Guanyin is neither male nore female, Chinese representations usually depict this bodhisattva as female.

The statue is about 1.5 metres tall. Although Guanyin is usually associated with Amituo Fo, in this case she is placed in front of the statue of Yaoshi Fo on the right side of the main altar for balance.

Guanyin's birthday is celebrated on the 19th day of the second lunar month. Her leaving home (or Great Renunciation) is celebrated on the 19th day of the sixth lunar month, and her enlightenment is celebrated on the 19th day of the ninth lunar month.

FOO DOG
← Detail

Carved, painted wood, about
10 centimetres high.

VICTORY BANNER
Detail →

Victory banners are always hung
in pairs. In this case, they are on
either side of the main altar.

This set is decorated with
homage to the Seven Buddhas of
the Auspicious Eon (Skt: *bhadra-kalpa*).

The two visible panels on the
right say:

NAMO PISAFO FO
NAMO SUCHI FO

The orange band around the
top is decorated with the Eight
Auspicious Symbols. Visible, from
left to right are: the two fishes,
royal parasol, lotus, Dharma
wheel, and conch shell.

Just visible at the bottom left
are stairs leading to the "Hall of
Virtue" chapel behind the main
altar.

Offering Table: In front of the main shrine is a wide offering table upon which are eight statues and a number of other small items. The order of the statues from left to right is always the same in every temple. In front of each statue is a glass oil lamp. These lights are one of the eight traditional Buddhist offerings.

Guan Yu Pusa
Dharma Protector

Pu Xian Pusa
Samantabhadra
Bodhisattva

Amituo Fo
Amitabha Buddha

Yaoshi Fo
Bhaisajyaguru
Buddha

Wenshu Pusa
Manjusri
Bodhisattva

Wei Tuo Pusa
Dharma Protector

Shi Jia Mou Ni Fo
Shakyamuni Buddha
Above: Meditation
Below: Parinirvana

Centre statues shown above larger for detail.
Actual sizes match others on table.

Guan Yu Pusa
Dharma Protector

Legend has it that Guan Yu was a famous general and hero from the Three Kingdoms Era of China, who was partially responsible for the collapse of the Han dynasty about 2000 years ago.

At the end of his long career, following many victories, he was captured, executed and beheaded. His severed head was returned to his leader, who buried it with full honours.

After his death, Guan Yu's ghost wandered the countryside calling out for the return of his head. His wandering eventually led him to Yuquan Hill about 350 years later, where the monk Zhiyi, founder of the Tientai School, was meditating. In life, Guan Yu had once been saved from an ambush by Pujing, an earlier incarnation of Zhiyi.

Now, Guan Yu's cries disturbed Zhiyi meditation. Finally, Zhiyi summoned the ghost and asked him: "Now you ask for your head, but where should all those you killed look for theirs?" At these words, Guan Yu repented his ways, took refuge, and sought Buddhist precepts and teachings from Zhiyi. Having entered the Bodhisattva path, his spirit thus became a Dharma Protector.

Guan Yu is depicted as a red-faced warrior with a full beard and a halberd (the Green Dragon Crescent Moon Blade). He is always shown on left of shrine. He is also known as Lord Guan, Lord of the Magnificent Beard, or (in Sanskrit) Sangharama Bodhisattva. His festival celebrated on the 13th day of the fifth lunar month.

PU XIAN PUSA
Samantabhadra
Universally Worthy Bodhisattva

Samantabhadra, the Universally Worthy, the All-Good Bodhisattva, is traditionally depicted on Buddha's right, seated on a white elephant. Here, he is shown in the attitude of princely repose, holding a long-stemmed lotus, a flower that grows a beautiful bloom from its roots in the mud. His left leg is in meditation pose, while his right leg is stepping down into the world, supported by a lotus pad.

In the Flower Garland (Ch: *Hua Yan Jing*; Skt: *Avatamsaka*) Sutra, Samantabhadra is recorded as having made Ten Great Bodhisattva Vows:
• To pay homage and respect to all Buddhas
• To praise all the Buddhas
• To make abundant offerings
• To repent misdeeds and evil karmas
• To rejoice in others' merits and virtues
• To request the Buddhas to continue teaching
• To request the Buddhas to remain in the world
• To follow the teachings of the Buddhas at all times
• To accommodate and benefit all living beings
• To transfer all merits and virtues to benefit all beings.

Samantabhadra is famously known for teaching the student Sudhana that wisdom only exists for the sake of putting it into practice; that it is only good insofar as it benefits all living beings. He is thus associated particularly with compassionate action, as opposed to Wenshu Pusa (Manjusri Bodhisattva), who is associated with wisdom and traditionally shown on Shakyamuni's left.

The festival of Samantabhadra is celebrated on the 21st day of second lunar month. His "home" is Emei, one of the four sacred Buddhist mountains of China, where many shrines are dedicated in his honour.

PU XIAN PUSA
Samantabhadra
Universally Worthy Bodhisattva
Detail

The statue, made in Taiwan in the Chinese artistic style, is burnished copper alloy, with three types of gold surface treatment, polychrome painted highlights on the head, and colourd glass jewel insets. The base is decorated with a lotus petal motif. It is about 25 cm tall.

AMITUO FO
Amitabha Buddha

After Shakyamuni, the historical Buddha, Amitabha is the most universally worshipped Buddha of the Mahayana and Vajrayana traditions. He is variously known as the Buddha of Infinite Light, the Buddha of Eternal Life and Lord of the Western Paradise. He is one of the five dhyani meditation Buddhas, residing in the Western Pure Land of Sukhavati, the Land of Ultimate Bliss. His colour is red and his symbol is the lotus.

Pure Land Buddhism is a major lineage in China, as well as in Viet Nam, Japan and Korea.

Amitabha is normally depicted with both hands in meditation pose, thumbs touching around a vase of elixir. In this rather unusual depiction on Shakyamuni's immediate right (our left), he is shown with his right hand in the gesture of giving — as part of this matched set of statues with Bhaisajyaguru, who is shown on Shakyamuni's immediate left, and whose left hand is extended. Amitabha's famous 48 Bodhisattva Vows include one which states that any living being who sincerely recites and holds in reverence His name just ten times will be reborn upon his death into Amitabha's Pure Land, where enlightenment may be achieved without hindrance or interference. In Chinese, this mantra is:

NAMO AMITUO FO

The Pure Land, and how to achieve it, are described in detail in the Amituo Jing (Skt: *Sukhavativyuha Sutra*), which is available freely on the internet, as well as in printed form from many Buddhist temples.

His festival is celebrated on the 7th day of eleventh lunar month.

Namo Amituo Fo, Namo Amituo Fo, Namo Amituo Fo.
Namo Amituo Fo, Namo Amituo Fo, Namo Amituo Fo.
Namo Amituo Fo, Namo Amituo Fo, Namo Amituo Fo.

YAOSHI FO
Bhaisajyaguru Buddha

Yaoshi Fo is variously known as Medicine Buddha, Medicine King Buddha and (like Shakyamuni) The Great Physician. He presides over the Pure Land known as Vaidūryanirbhāsa, or "Pure Lapis Lazuli." His colour is deep blue and his symbol is a pagoda or jewel box filled with healing herbs.

The Twelve Vows of the Medicine Buddha upon attaining Enlightenment, according to the Medicine Buddha Sutra are:
• To illuminate countless realms with his radiance, enabling anyone to become a Buddha just like him
• To awaken the minds of sentient beings through his light of lapis lazuli
• To provide the sentient beings with whatever material needs they require
• To correct heretical views and inspire beings toward the path of the Bodhisattva
• To help beings follow the Moral Precepts, even if they failed before.
• To heal beings born with deformities, illness or other physical sufferings
• To help relieve the destitute and the sick
• To help women who wish to be reborn as men achieve their desired rebirth
• To help heal mental afflictions and delusions
• To help the oppressed be free from suffering
• To relieve those who suffer from terrible hunger and thirst
• To help clothe those who are destitute and suffering from cold and mosquitoes.

Bhaisajyaguru's mantra is:

OM BHAISAJYE BHAISAJYE
MAHABHAISAJYA
BHAISAJYE RAZA
SAMUDGATE SVAHA

He is usually depicted with his left hand holding a medicine jar in his lap and with his right hand palm up on his knee, holding a fruit or flower. In this rather unusual depiction on Shakyamuni's immediate left (our right), he is shown with his left hand in the gesture of giving — as part of this matched set of statues with Amitabha, shown on Shakyamuni's immediate right, whose left hand is extended.

His festival is celebrated on the 13th day of ninth lunar month.

YAOSHI FO
Bhaisajyaguru Buddha
Medicine Buddha
Detail

Wenshu Pusa
Manjusri
Gentle Glory Bodhisattva

Manjusri, the Bodhisattva of Wisdom, is traditionally depicted on the Buddha's left, seated on a lion. Here, he is shown in the attitude of princely repose, holding a ruler's sceptre. His right leg is in meditation pose, while his left leg is stepping down into the world, supported by a lotus pad. His mantra is:

OM AH RA PA CHA NA DHIH

Manusri is famously known in the Lotus Sutra (Ch: *Fa Hua Jing*; Skt: *Saddharma Pundarika*) for leading the Naga (dragon) King's daughter to enlightenment. In the tantric tradition he is shown holding in his right hand the flaming sword of discriminating wisdom to cut through ignorance, and in his left hand a sacred book, the Perfection of Wisdom Sutra (Ch: *Bore Bouomiduo*; Skt: *Prajna Paramita*).

Manusri is often highlighted on the first day of the lunar New Year, but his special day is celebrated on the fourth day of the fourth month, according to the lunar calendar. His "home" is Wutai Shan, one of the four sacred Buddhist mountains of China, where many shrines are dedicated in his honour. It is located in Shanxi Province, in the north-east.

WENSHU PUSA
Manjusri
Gentle Glory Bodhisattva
Another view

WEI TUO PUSA
Dharma Protector

Legend has it that Wei Tuo is a soldier of the Northern Heavenly King and commander-in-chief of the 32 Heavenly Generals who serve the Heavenly Kings of the Four Directions.

Once, in his previous life at the time of Shakyamuni Buddha in India, he was known by the name Skanda, and he was the son of a devoted Buddhist king. Before Shakyamuni Buddha passed away, he instructed Skanda to protect and preserve the Dharma teachings. After the Buddha's pari-nirvana, demons stole his relics. Wei Tuo fought the demons and returned the Dharma relics to their rightful place. For this reason, he is depicted as a general with a tall helmet and golden chainmail armour. His belt is decorated with a monster's head.

His particular tasks have been to protect the purity of members of the sangha community and to resolve disputes between sangha members.

In Chinese temples, he is always shown on the right side of the shrine. Sometimes he is shown facing the shrine itself as a representation of his commitment to the Buddha. His image is also often found at the end of Chinese Buddhist texts.

Wei Tuo's festival is celebrated on the third day of the sixth lunar month.

Guan Yu Pusa
Dharma Protector

This larger version is situated high above the floor to the left of the main shrine as you face it. (*See page 2*)

The statue is made of wood with gold and polychrome paint. It is about one meter tall.

Beneath it is a door leading to the chapel behind the main shrine.

WEI TUO PUSA
Dharma Protector

This larger version is situated on a shelf, high above the floor to the right of the main shrine as you face it. (*See page 2*)

The statue is made of wood with gold and polychrome paint. It is about one meter tall.

Like the statue of Guan Yu on the other side of the room, it has an honourific roof above it.

INCENSE OFFERING IMPLEMENTS

Main Altar

The incense burner in the centre is topped with a lion.

On the left at the front is a small bowl of wood shavings. Behind that are a small brass vase and a small bowl of sand.

On the right at the front is a small bowl of powdered incense. Behind that is a glass vase with a pair of brass chopsticks and a white metal poker topped with a wing design.

The lacquer tray is about 30 centimetres wide. It sits at the base of the main altar, directly behind the lectern. Above it you can see one of three water offerings in front of the 36 oil lamps that line the stepped shelves in front of the main altar.

Musical Instruments

These two percussion instruments, the wooden fish and the bronze bell bowl, are staples of the Chinese Buddhist liturgical service.

The fish is used to mark the beat of chanting, and the gong is used to signal the beginning, the end, or a particular key phrase (for example when one is expected to bow).

They are placed on the left and right of the shrine, respectively, flanking the lectern used by the master of ceremonies.

Muyu
Wooden Fish

This instrument comes in all sizes. The sound chamber is round, carved with a handle depicting two fish embracing a pearl in their mouths. Muyu are also used in Korean and Japanese Mahayana Buddhism.

The fish represents wakefulness, since fish don't sleep (at least in the sense we normally think of it). Thus it is considered a useful motif for monks and nuns to remember.

Luo
Bell Bowl

Gongs, like bells in general, are usually made of cast bronze. The main determinant of the note is the size of the bowl, but fine tuning is achieved by hammering (which also serves a decorative purpose).

This bell has been lacquered as well. The sound is achieved by striking the upper edge with a mallet wrapped in cloth.

DRAGON DRUM
→ This portable percussion centre is used to provide counterpoints during chanting.

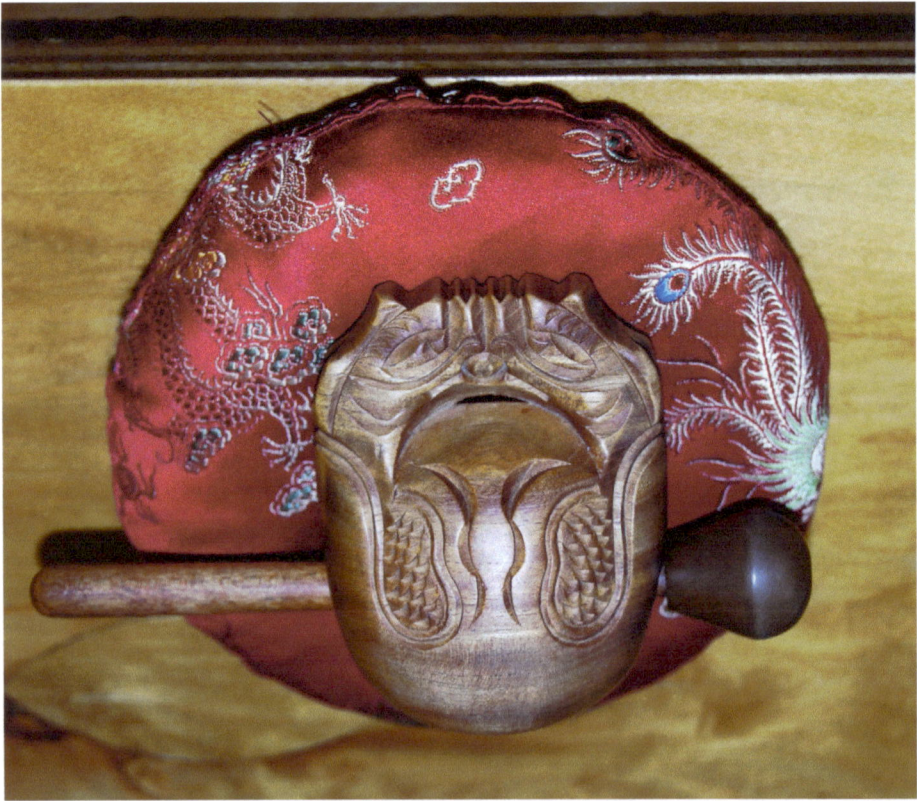

SMALL WOODEN FISH
↓ This hand-held percussion instrument is used to keep time during chanting.

GUANYIN
Avalokitesvara
Bodhisattva of Compassion

This altar is just to the right of the main entrance at the back of the shrine hall.

The large statue in the back is Guanyin, depicted with a thousand hands and a thousand eyes. It is said that when Guanyin experienced the intensity of the suffering of the triple world, she spontaneously manifested in a thousand forms to assist all beings. Each hand holds an implement associated with a particular type of compassionate action.

Guanyin is often depicted holding a lotus. The shrine cabinet depicts a carved mature lotus blossom at the top centre, above a title scroll which reads:

> THE COMPASSIONATE ONE
> WHO CROSSES ALL BEINGS
> OVER THE OCEAN OF SUFFERING

On the left side pillar of the cabinet are ideograms for a poem which reads:

> SUBLIME, MAGNIFICENT, MERITORIOUS AND WISE,
> THE BODHISATTVA'S INNUMERABLE WONDROUS ACTS
> LEAD SENTIENT BEINGS FROM SUFFERINGS
> TO PERFECTION IN WISDOM

On the right side pillar of the cabinet are ideograms for a poem which reads:

> THE IMAGE OF GOODNESS, KINDNESS AND COMPASSION
> THAT IS THE BODHISATTVA GUANYIN
> CAME ABOUT AFTER EONS OF PRACTICES;
> AS THE RESULTING MERITS AND VIRTUES
> PERVADE COUNTLESS WORLDS,
> SENTIENT BEINGS ASPIRE FOR HER BLESSINGS
> AND PROTECTION TO ESCAPE CALAMITY AND DISASTER

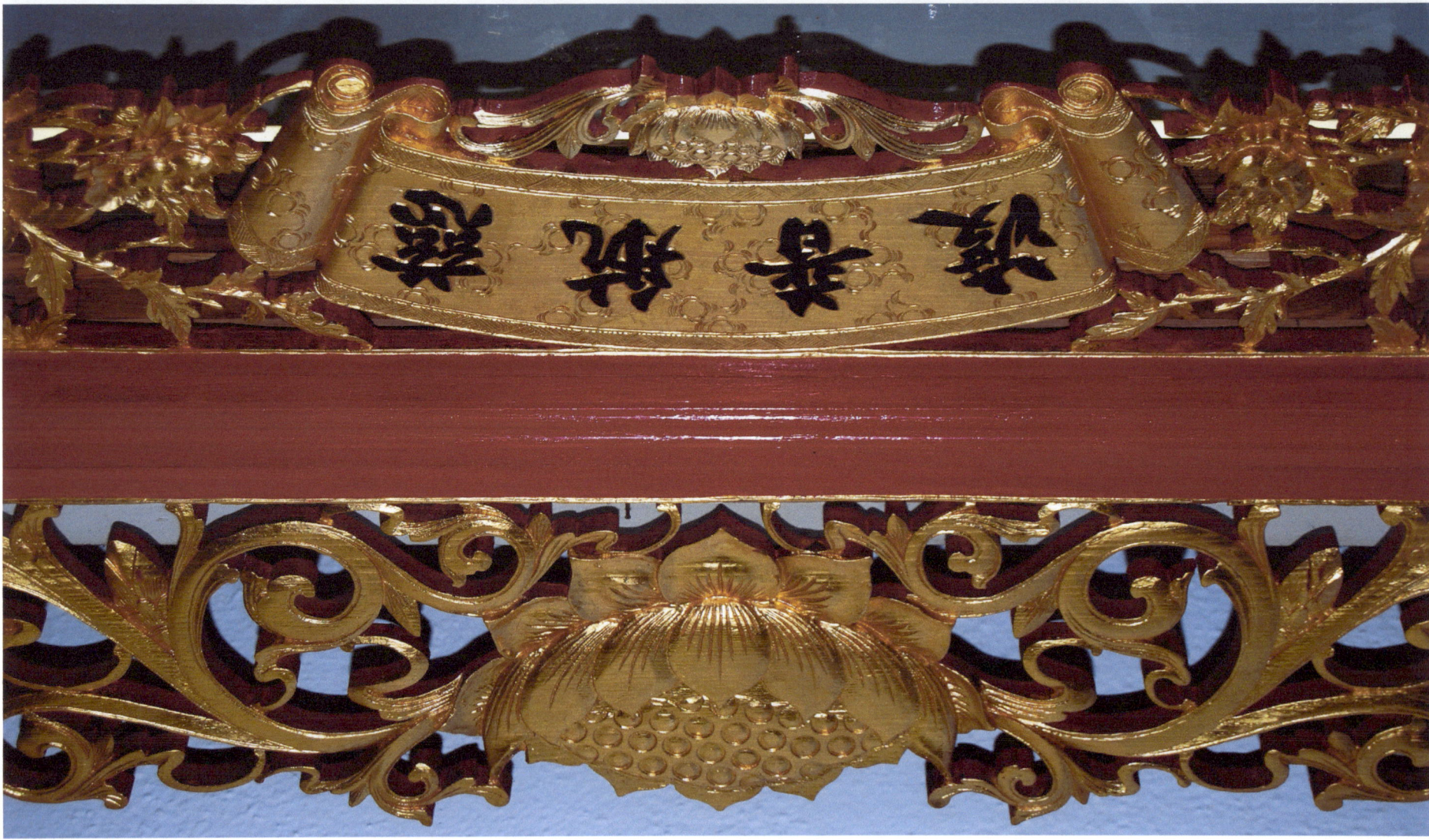

The Three Venerable Ones

The three figures shown in front of the large Guanyin statues are a trio that are frequently shown together. This is a very common shrine in Chinese Buddhist temples.

On the left is Lung Nu, the Dragon's grand-daughter. Legend has it that once upon a time Guanyin rescued the son of one of the Dragon Kings. In gratitude, the Dragon King sent his grand-daughter to bestow the Pearl of Light on Guanyin. When Lung Nu saw Guanyin, she was inspired to become her disciple. Guanyin accepted her request with the qualification that she continue to be the keeper of the Pearl of Light (represented here by a vase).

In the front centre is Guanyin. This particular statue is said to be more than 200 years old. It is made of wood with gold paint and comes from north of Shanghai. The temple purchased it from a vendor at the Canadian National Exhibition.

On the right is Shan Cai, also known as the Child of Wealth, or Sudhana in Sanskrit. He is the main protagonist in the penultimate chapter of the Avatamsaka Sutra. He also appears in the Gandavyuha Sutra as a seeker of enlightenment who requested teachings from many Buddhas and Bodhisattvas. His association with Guanyin and Lung Nu comes primarily from the Ming dynasty text: *The Complete Tale of Guanyin and the Southern Seas*.

The Three Venerable Ones
Detail

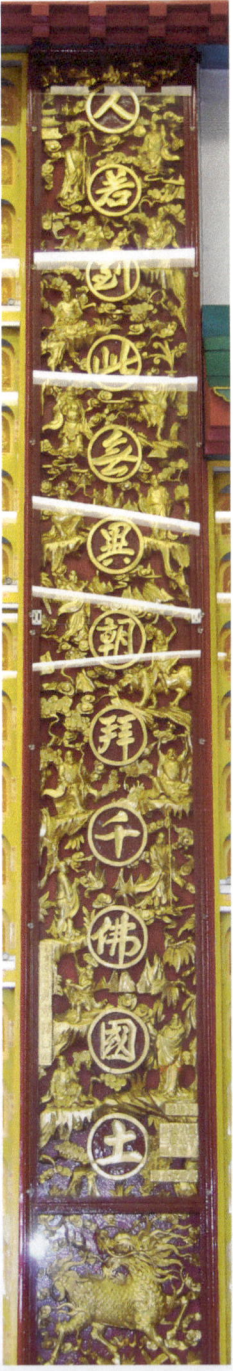

Memorial Wall

A large section of the temple wall is taken up with permanent memorials. Each alcove contains a small bas relief image of Shi Jia Mou Ni Fo, a loved one's name, and a small lamp. The lamps were traditionally kept lit at all times, but in contemporary usage are lit only on Sundays for a food offering service (as a gesture of environmental sustainability).

Left Memorial Pillar

The words read:

If you come here
it is equal to
paying respect
to all temples
of the ten directions

Right Memorial Pillar

The words read:

If people come here
to worship
it is equal to
worshipping the
BuddhaRealm of the
Thousand Buddhas

The Thousand Buddha Remembrance Wall

Detail

MEMORIAL WALL, REAR CHAPEL

Small plaques are dedicated to the memory of loved ones.

The statue is Dayuan Dizang Pusa, Ksitigarbha Bodhisattva, also know as Earth Store Bodhisattva. His unique vow was to take responsibility for the salvation of all beings after the parinirvana of Shakyamuni until Maitreya, the future Buddha, arrives. He is also often associated with the salvation of beings suffering in the Hells. His festival is celebrated on the 30th day of seventh lunar month.

The ideograms on the offering box under the incense burner say:

OFFERING BOX FOR

SOWING SEEDS

BROADLY CULTIVATING

THE FIELD OF MERITS

DAYUAN DIZANG PUSA
Ksitigarbha Bodhisattva
Earth Store Bodhisattva
Alternate views

DAYUAN DIZANG PUSA
Ksitigarbha Bodhisattva
Earth Store Bodhisattva

These statues are in front of another section of the remembrance wall, yet to be filled. The small metal statue in front is about 25 years old and comes from Taiwan. The inscription on the base says:

NAMO DAYUAN DIZANG PUSA

The larger statue in the back is made of polychromed wood. It comes from southern China and is also about 25 years old.

The two small statues on either side are made of cast iron, and they also represent Dayuan Dizang, shown as a monk. He is traditionally depicted thus, holding a staff in his right hand to break open the gates of Hell, and a wish fulfilling gem in his left to light up the darkness. These statues were made in Japan, and were left at the door of the temple by an anonymous patron several years ago. They are each about 9 centimetres high.

YAOSHI FO, OFFERINGS AND THE REMEMBRANCE WALL IN THE REAR SHRINE
Overleaf →

Behind the main altar is a small chapel with a remembrance wall. The statue is Yaoshi Fo (Bhaisajyaguru, Medicine Buddha). On the next page is a picture.

SHI JIA MOU NI FO
SHAKYAMUNI BUDDHA

← This white stone statue of Shakyamuni in the gesture of "Calling the Earth to Witness" is on the left side wall of the chapel behind the main altar, and sits about one metre tall. It is of Chinese origin and was donated to the temple by members of the congregation.

Note the lion's head emerging from the lotus throne. That's a very unusual depiction.

GUAN YU PUSA
Dharma Protector →

This wooden statue stands in the far left corner of the rear chapel. It is about one metre tall.

Offering Table: This offering table is dedicated to Guanyin, shown in the picture in the centre of the table in an alternate manifestation known as King of Ghosts. It is just inside the front door of the temple, on the right. This was a temporary altar erected on the back wall beside the Guanyin shrine for the annual Ching Ming Ancestor Remembrance Ceremony. The photo at the top left shows the ordination of Ven. Wu De. The pink poster at the top right is soliciting funds for Ching Kwok's sister temple in Edmonton.

OFFERINGS FOR THE DECEASED

Incense is offered and slips of paper with the names of the recently deceased are posted on the right wall of the temple, under a picture of Amituo Fo.

This was a temporary altar erected for the annual Ching Ming service.

Gold and red are traditional colours of respect and good fortune. The ideograms on the offering table under the incense burner say:

DONATION BOX FOR
INCENSE AND LAMP OIL

GUANYIN AND SEVERAL DHARMA SAYINGS

These pictures are just to the left of the Guanyin shrine in the back corner of the temple beside the entrance.

THE VIRTUE OF ENLIGHTENMENT
("KWOK") AND THE VINAYA CODE
OF BEHAVIOUR ILLUSTRATE THE
CHARACTER OF THE SCHOOL

GUANYIN
Bodhisattva of Compassion

COMPLETE ("CHING")
REALIZATIONS COME FROM THE
TEACHINGS OF SUPREME TEACHERS

若真修道人
常自見己過
不說他人非
與道即相應

True practitioners
Always see their own faults.
Not to speak ill of others —
that is in unison with the path.

千江有水千江月
萬里無雲萬里天
千處祈求千處應
苦海常作渡人舟

With a thousand lakes,
there will be a thousand reflections of the moon;
With ten thousand miles of cloudlessness,
there is the ten thousand miles of the sky.
The prayers from a thousand places
are each answered in those thousand places;
One always be the raft for others
in the sea of suffering.

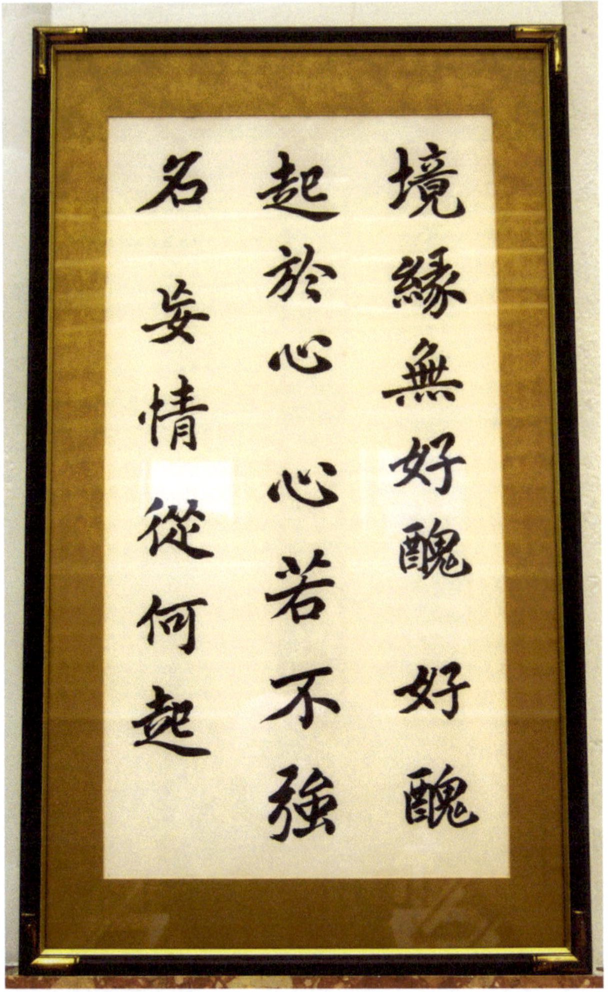

境緣無好醜
好醜起於心
心若不強名
妄情從何起

There is nothing good or ugly about objects;
All goodness and ugliness arise from the mind.
If the mind does not discriminate,
Where can deceitful motivations come from?

功德堂

HALL OF VIRTUE

This sign hangs over the stairway on the left side of
the main shrine, leading to the rear chapel.

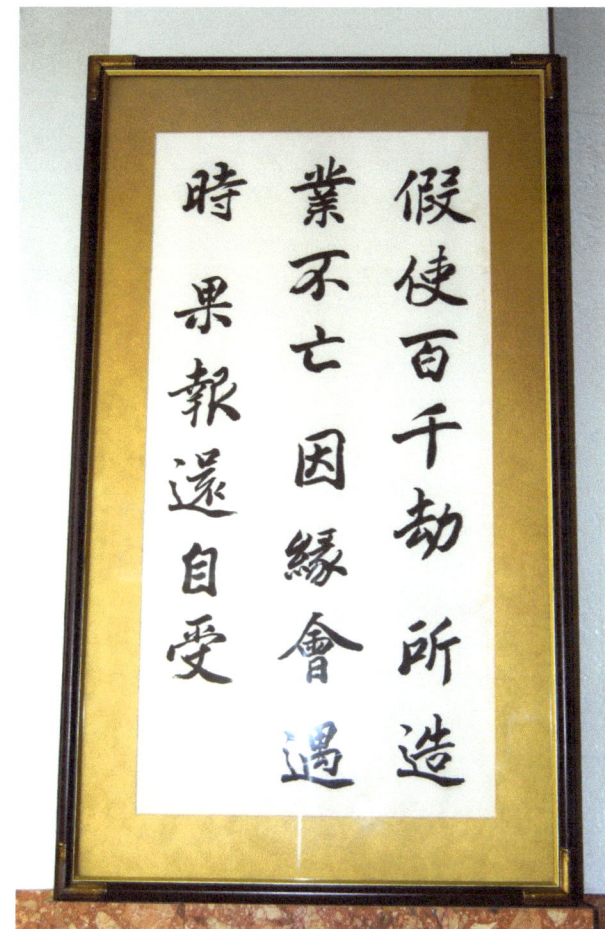

梵剎莊嚴
佛日增輝

THE REALM OF BUDDHAHOOD IS MAGNIFICENT;
THE SUN OF THE BUDDHAS INCREASES ITS SPLENDOR.

假使百千劫所造
業不亡因緣會遇
時果報還自受

EVEN THROUGH TENS OF THOUSANDS OF EONS,
THE KARMA ONE HAS COMMITTED REMAINS UNDIMINISHED.
WHEN THE CAUSE MEETS WITH THE CONDITIONS,
ONE STILL HAS TO EXPERIENCE THE KARMIC FRUITS.

THE WESTERN PURE LAND OF AMITUO FO: Amituo Fo is accompanied by his two chief disciples, the Bodhisattvas Guanyin on his right and Da Shi Zi (Skt: *Mahasthamaprapta,* Arrival of Great Strength) on his left. They are surrounded by a retinue of practitioners and devotees within a palace surrounded by a lotus pond. Amituo Fo sits under a royal parasol. The panel is approximately two meters high and five-and-a-half meters wide. It sits above the windows on the south wall.

SHI JIA MOU NI BUDDHA PREACHING THE DHARMA: The Buddha is surrounded by his chief disciples, a retinue of Arhats, Bodhisattvas and saints, and the Four Kings of Sumeru. The panel is approximately two meters high and five-and-a-half meters wide. It sits above the windows on the south wall, to the right of the Pure Land panel.

MAIN SHRINE ROOM: This photo was taken from in front of the altar. We are facing east. On the far left is the edge of the memorial wall. In the back left corner, you can see the Guanyin shrine. In the back centre, you can see an incense offering table directly in front of the entrance. The old theatre balcony is used as a library. In the back right corner is a small information booth.

The balcony houses a reference library containing the Three Baskets of Buddhist Teachings (Skt. *Tripitaka* – Sutras, Abhidharma and Vinaya). The large bell upstairs on the left was cast in Taiwan for the inauguration of the temple, emblazoned with the names of the four main Bodhisattvas, two poems, the temple name and the inauguration date. On the right is a large drum. In traditional temples in China, the bell and then the drum are sounded each morning. In the evening the drum and then the bell are sounded. However, they are so loud that here they are only used on special occasions.

MAIN OFFERING TABLE: This photo was taken at the back of the main hall, looking east toward Bathurst Street, directly inside the front door of the temple. The table is about one-and-a-half meters high and three metres across. It serves as a location where visitors can place offerings of fruit, and so on; it also controls the *feng shui* energy in the room. In this photograph, the temporary Ching Ming altar to the left of the door (shown in other photos) has been replaced by a small lending library.

The table is wood, polychrome and gold, illustrated with lions on the four corners, and scenes from the life of the Buddha around the upper sides. These upper panels are part of a set with the panels in the bases of the large statues on the main altar, as well as other *bas relief* panels in the temple.

FRONT FACADE

The front facade of the building has been modified to its current use with the addition of pillars and a Chinese-style ceramic roof cornice and portico.

The figures along the roof line are auspicious animals which represent the forces of nature: Fire, Wind, Rain, Thunder, Lightning, and so on. In the Chinese folk tradition, they are there to protect the building from being damaged by those forces.